You're in the Band

Book 1

For Lead Guitar

TAB EDITION

by Dave Clo

ISBN-13: 978-1-4234-1638-8
ISBN-10: 1-4234-1638-4

Dave Clo: Guitars, Bass and keyboards
Tim Clo: Drums
Chris Dauphin: Keyboards

WILLIS MUSIC

Exclusively Distributed By

HAL•LEONARD®
CORPORATION
7777 W. BLUEMOUND RD. P.O. BOX 13819
MILWAUKEE, WISCONSIN 53213

Cover Photo by Timothy Clo

Adplate photos used by permission of
jj@astartledchameleon.co.uk

Visit Hal Leonard Online at
www.halleonard.com

Congratulations! We've talked it over and decided "You're In The Band"!
Here is a list of the songs you will need to learn. When you can play your part with the rehearsal track without any mistakes, write the 'date mastered' to the right of the rehearsal track number. When you have perfected a song with the performance track, write in the date next to its track number. GET BUSY! We have our first show in about six months!

Song Index

Song	Page	Rehearsal Track #	Date Mastered	Performance Track #	Date Mastered
Grung-E	6	2	_____	3	_____
E-mail	7	4	_____	5	_____
Two Down	8	6	_____	7	_____
Phrygian Sea	9	8	_____	9	_____
The Gauge	10	10	_____	11	_____
Graduation	11	12	_____	13	_____
Forthright?	12	14	_____	15	_____
Pentatonic	13	16	_____	17	_____
Out on a Ledger	14	18	_____	19	_____
A Minor Setback	15	20	_____	21	_____
Surf String	16	22	_____	23	_____
Upshot	17	24	_____	25	_____
The Gauge 2	18	26	_____	27	_____
Geology II	19	28	_____	29	_____
Pentatonic 2	20	30	_____	31	_____
Out on a Ledger 2	21	32	_____	33	_____
Grung-E (Solo)	24	34	_____	35	_____
Two Down (Solo)	25	36	_____	37	_____
Phygian Sea (Solo)	26	38	_____	39	_____
The Guage (Solo)	27	40	_____	41	_____
Forthright (Solo)	28	42	_____	43	_____
Out on a Ledger (Solo)	29	44	_____	45	_____
Surf String (Solo)	30	46	_____	47	_____
Geology II (Solo)	31	48	_____	49	_____

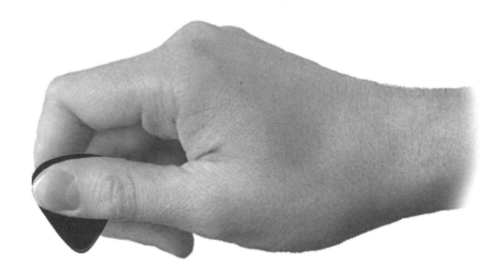

The pick should be held between the thumb and the index finger. Use only a downward motion when plucking the string until 8th notes are introduced on page 9.

WHAT'S THAT CALLED?

the body   the neck   the head

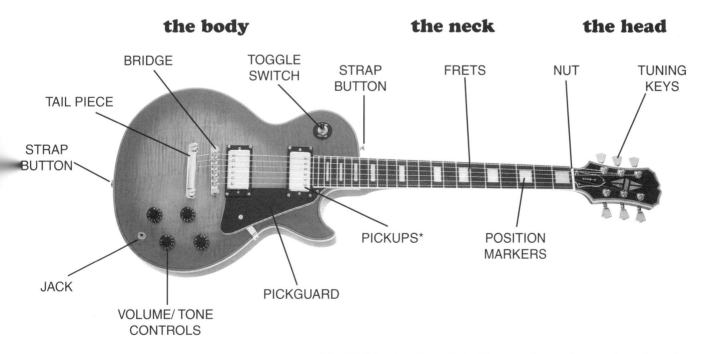

BRIDGE   TOGGLE SWITCH   STRAP BUTTON   FRETS   NUT   TUNING KEYS

TAIL PIECE

STRAP BUTTON

JACK

VOLUME/ TONE CONTROLS

PICKGUARD

PICKUPS*

POSITION MARKERS

*ACOUSTIC GUITARS HAVE A "SOUND HOLE" INSTEAD OF PICKUPS.

Tuning the guitar can be very difficult for a beginner. Try to tune with the "tuning track" (track 1 of your CD), or with an electronic tuner until you are ready to tune the guitar on your own. Track 1 of the CD contains each string played 3 three times, starting with string # 1 (E).

open notes

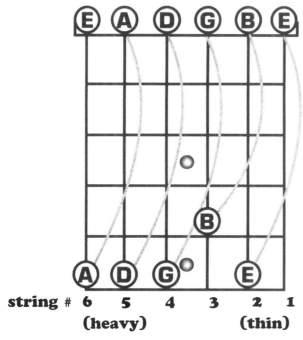

string # 6 5 4 3 2 1
(heavy)   (thin)

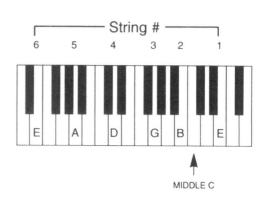

Once you are comfortable with the idea of tuning the guitar by yourself, follow these steps:

1. **TUNE THE FIRST STRING OPEN (pluck the string without pressing any frets) TO AN "E". Use a pitch pipe, tuning fork, piano or any reliable source.**

2. **MATCH THE "E" ON THE 5th FRET OF THE 2nd STRING TO SOUND LIKE THE 1st STRING OPEN.**

3. **MATCH THE "B" ON THE 4th FRET OF THE 3rd STRING TO SOUND LIKE THE 2nd STRING OPEN.**

4. **MATCH THE "G" ON THE 5th FRET OF THE 4th STRING TO SOUND LIKE THE 3rd STRING OPEN.**

5. **MATCH THE "D" ON THE 5th FRET OF THE 5th STRING TO SOUND LIKE THE 4th STRING OPEN.**

6. **MATCH THE "A" ON THE 5th FRET OF THE 6th STRING TO SOUND LIKE THE 5th STRING OPEN.**

7. **PLAY YOUR GUITAR. IT SHOULD BE IN TUNE.**

These CD icons contain the track numbers for your 'Rehearsal' and 'Performance' for each new piece.

WHAT IS GUITAR TAB?

First of all, it is very important to make it clear that using guitar tab is the easiest way to learn new material but in the long run it is still very important to learn to <u>read music</u> and to learn <u>music theory</u>.

See **You're In the Band – Lead Guitar** or **"Unplugged"** to learn to read music.

See **You're In the Band – Rhythm Guitar** to learn music theory.

Guitar "tab" which is short for "tablature" is so easy because it shows you what to play. There are 6 lines and each one represents a different guitar string.

The top line is the thinnest string (1st string) and the bottom line is the heavy string (6th string). It creates a picture of an upside down guitar but gives somewhat the view from the player's perspective.

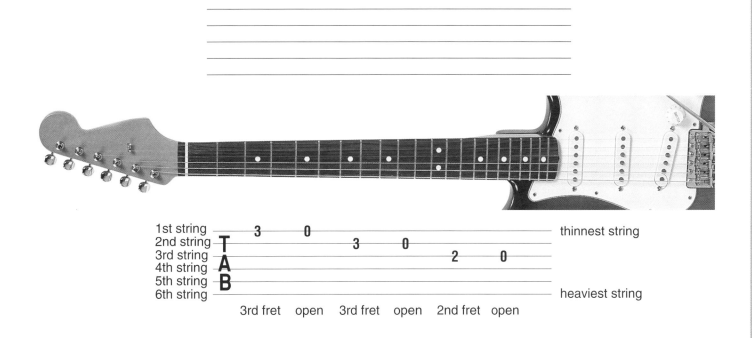

Rhythm

First is shown how rhythms are written in regular music notation and then with guitar tab.

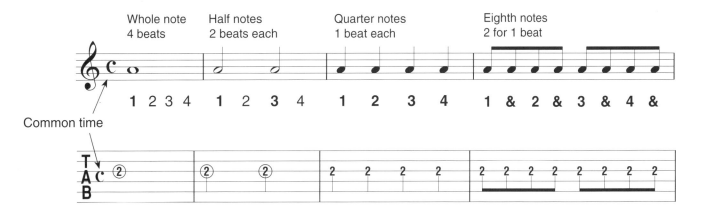

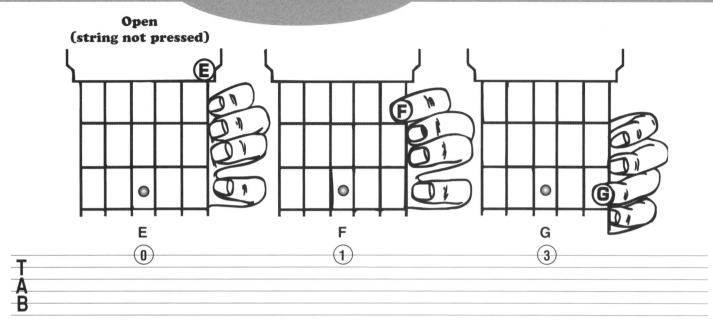

To play E: Pluck down on the 1st string (smallest string) open. *
To play F: Place the 1st finger (index) on the 1st fret of this string.**
To play G: Place the 3rd finger (ring) on the 3rd fret of this string.**

GRUNG-E

Chords are for Rhythm player

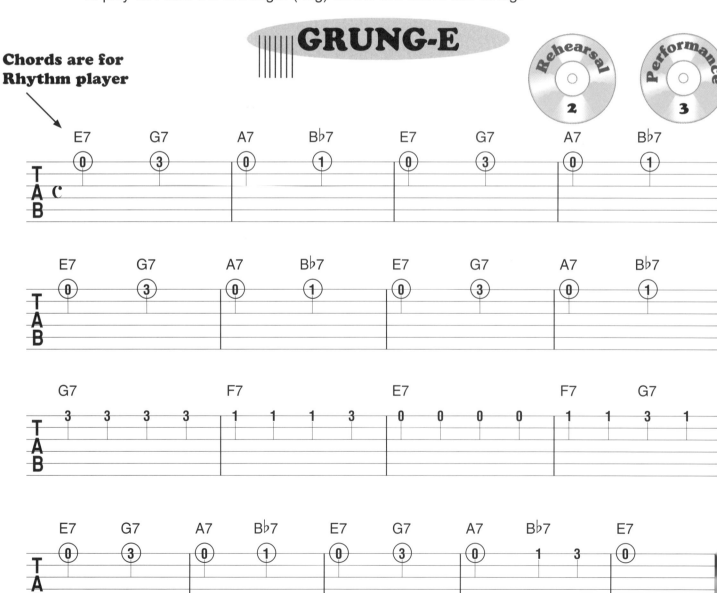

* Open means to pluck the string without pressing any frets.   *** The term "on the fret" really means next to the fret as pictured.*

E-MAIL

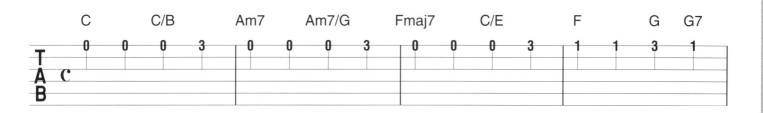

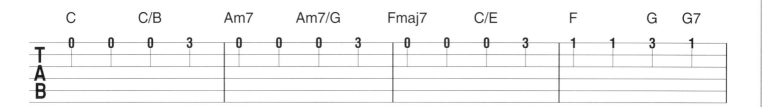

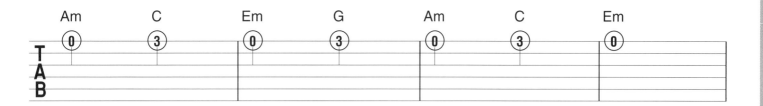

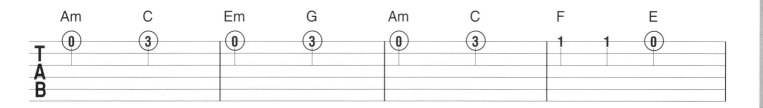

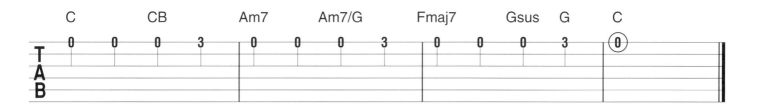

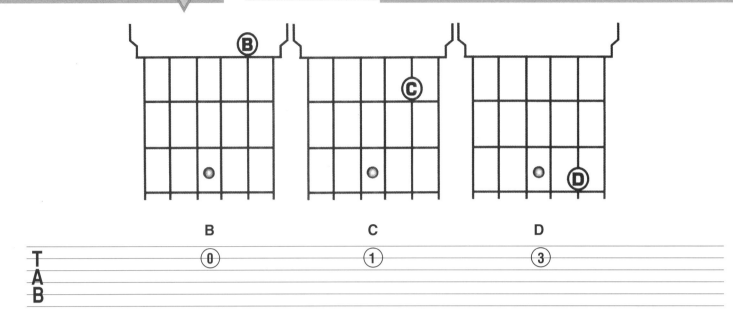

To play B: Pluck the 2nd string open.
To play C: Place the 1st finger on the 1st fret of this string.
To play D: Place the 3rd finger on the 3rd fret of this string.

TWO DOWN

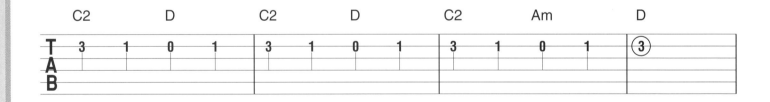

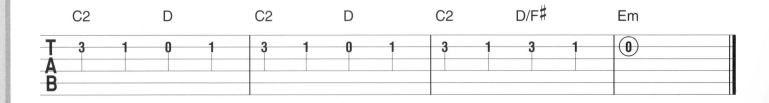

PLAYING EIGHTH NOTES

When playing 8th notes, the picking hand does not change speed. By plucking down and up instead of just down, you double the amount of times the string is hit without increasing your hand speed.

⊓ **DOWN PICK**

∨ **UP-PICK**

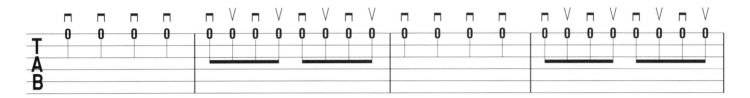

PHRYGIAN SEA

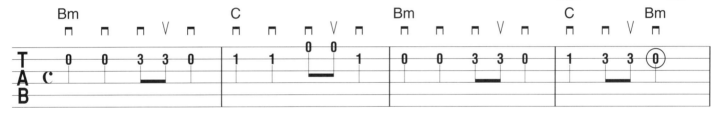

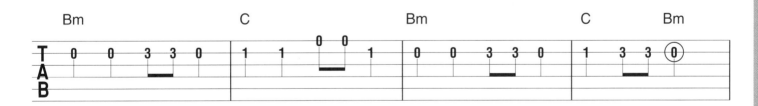

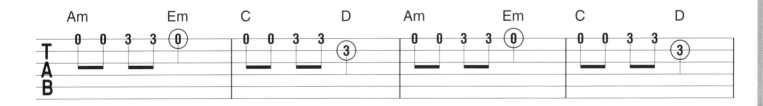

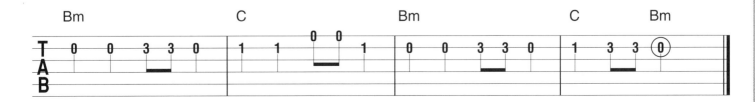

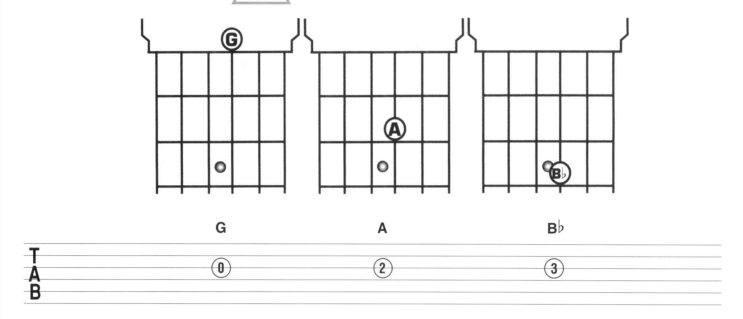

To play G: Pluck the third string open.
To play A: Place the 2nd finger on the 2nd fret of this string.
To play B♭ (B flat): Place the 3rd finger on the 3rd fret of this string.

THE GAUGE

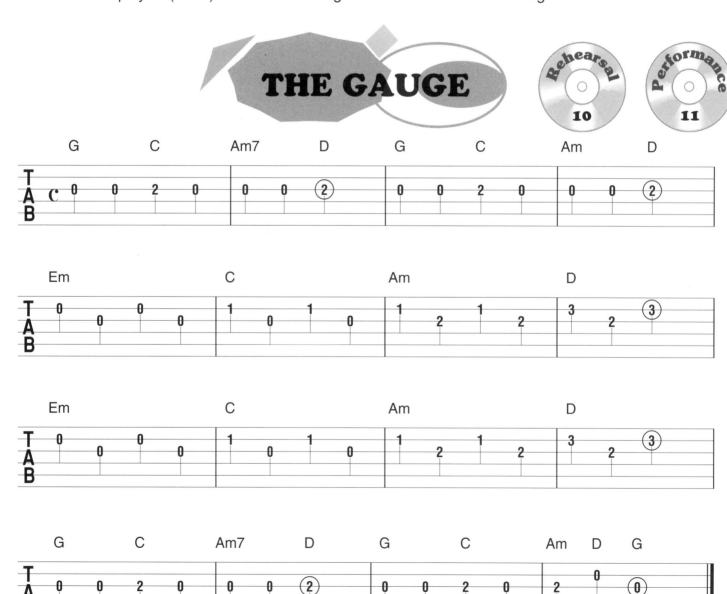

GRADUATION

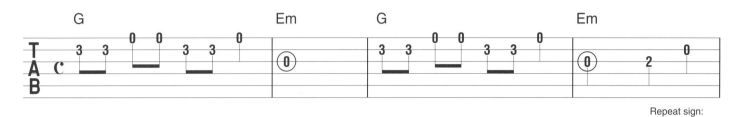

Repeat sign:
Go back to
the beginning

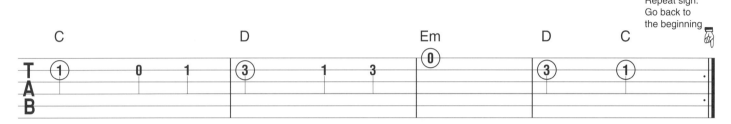

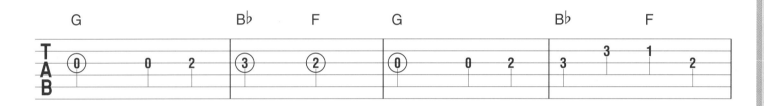

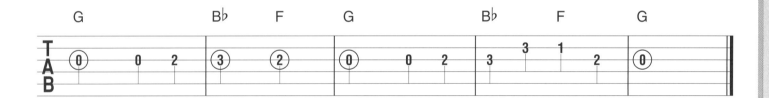

Try These Two Scales

Play with quarter notes and then 8th notes.

This one is called G Mixolydian

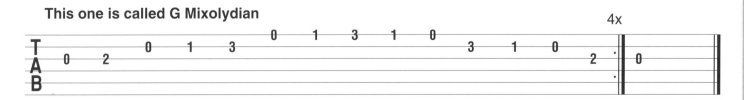

This one is called G Dorian

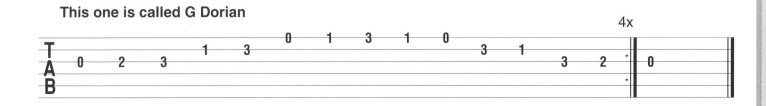

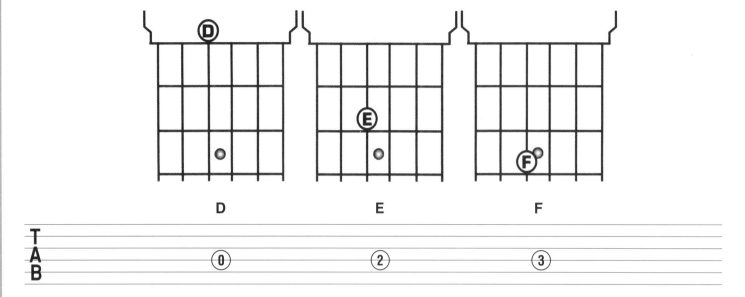

D E F

To play D: Pluck the 4th string open.
To play E: Place the 2nd finger on the 2nd fret of this string.
To play F: Place the 3rd finger on the 3rd fret of this string.

FORTHRIGHT?

Rehearsal 14

Performance 15

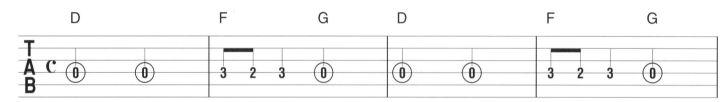

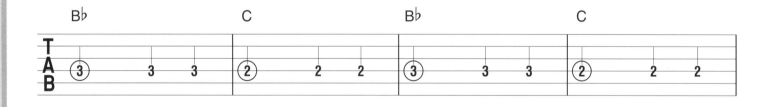

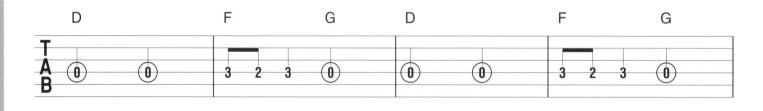

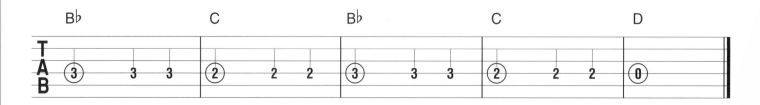

RHYTHM

Rests: Silence any ringing notes.

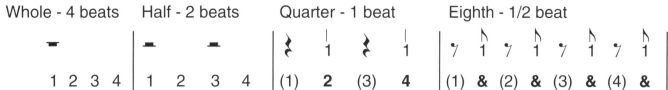

PENTATONIC

NOTES ON THE FIFTH STRING

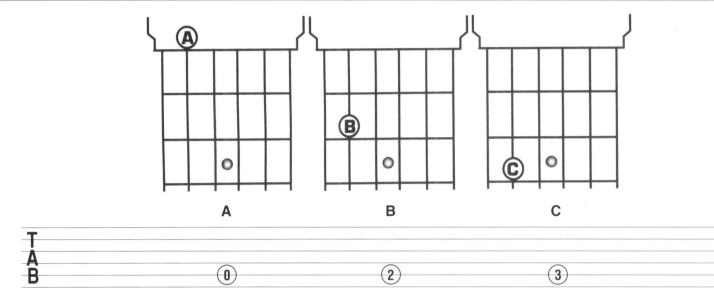

To play A: Pluck the 5th string open.
To play B: Place the 2nd finger on the 2nd fret of this string.
To play C: Place the 3rd finger on the 3rd fret of this string.

OUT ON A LEDGER

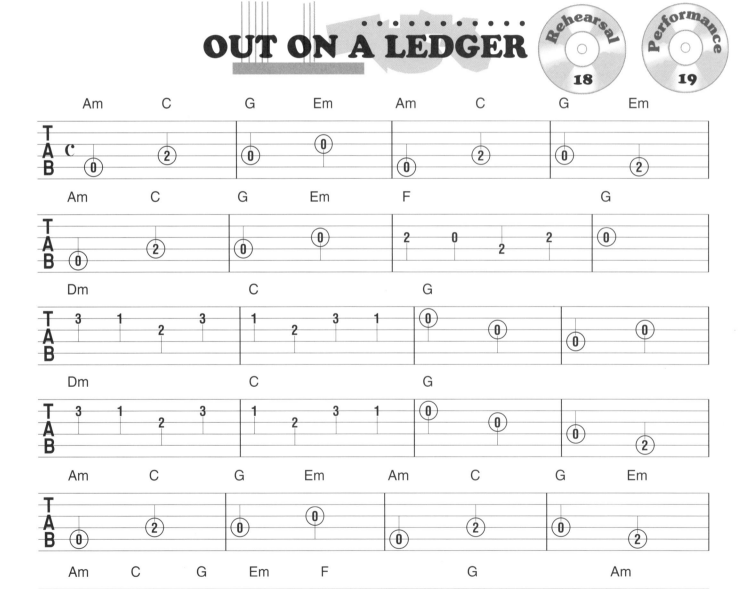

A MINOR SETBACK

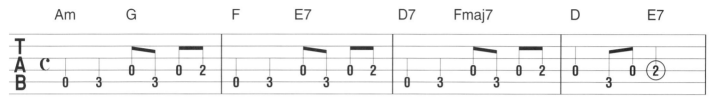

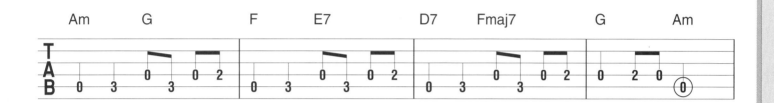

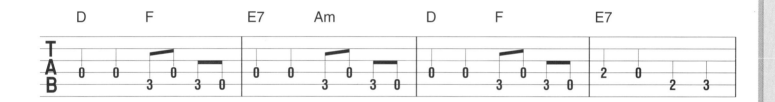

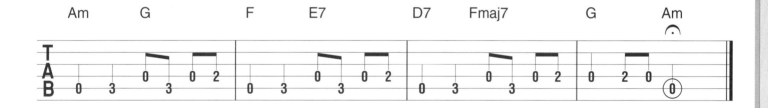

HIGH A (ON THE 1ST STRING)

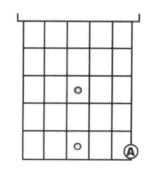

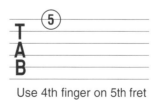

Use 4th finger on 5th fret

The A Minor Scale (2 octaves)

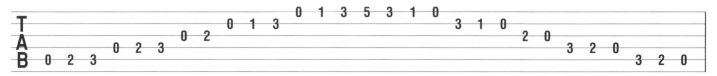

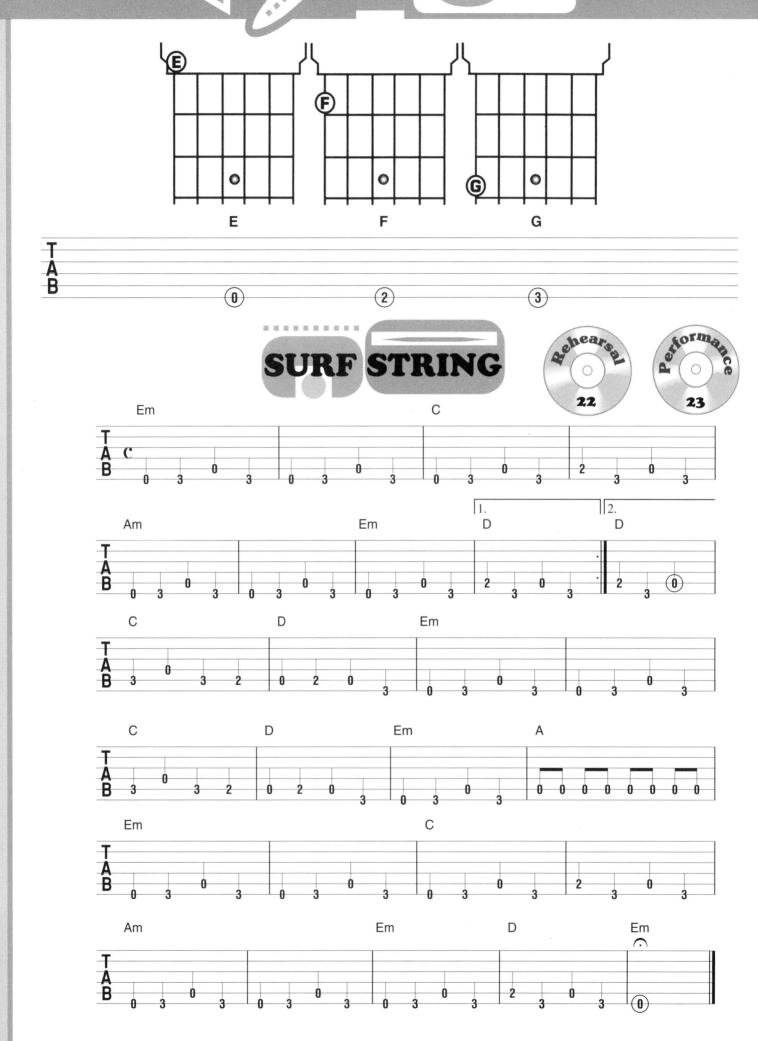

SURF STRING

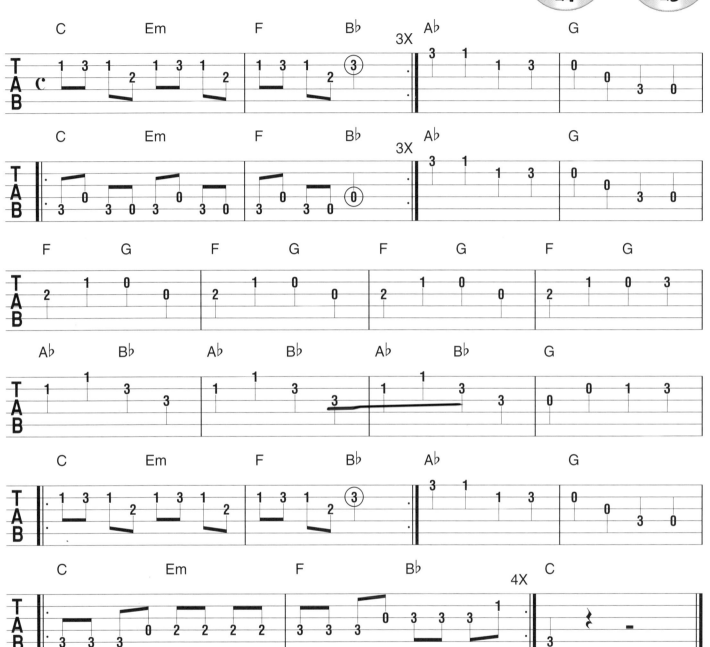

19 NOTE REVIEW

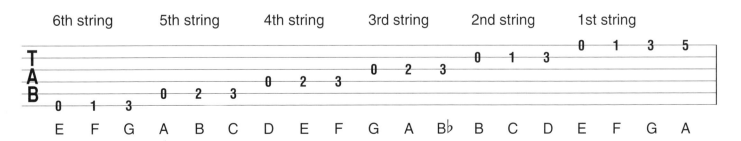

FACT FILE

F Sharp (written F#) is one fret higher than F. There are 3 F#'s in the open position of the guitar.

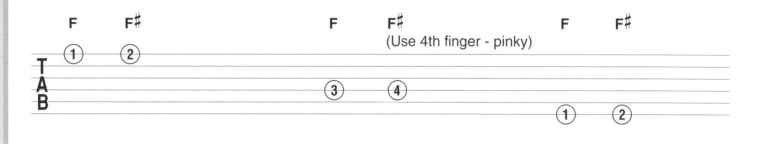

(Use 4th finger - pinky)

THE GAUGE 2

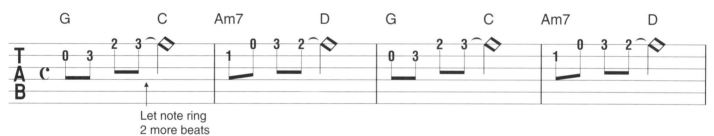

Let note ring
2 more beats

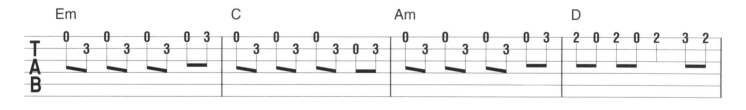

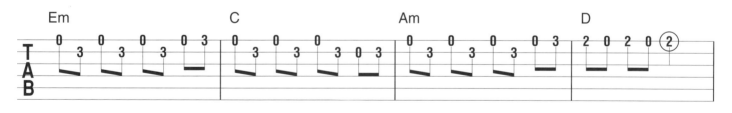

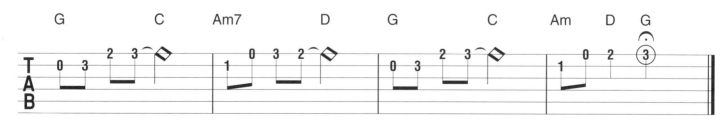

16th Note Rhythms

Sixteenth notes are twice as fast as eighth notes, and the picking hand must move twice the speed. Eighth note sections are usually played with all down-strokes, once 16th notes are introduced in a piece.

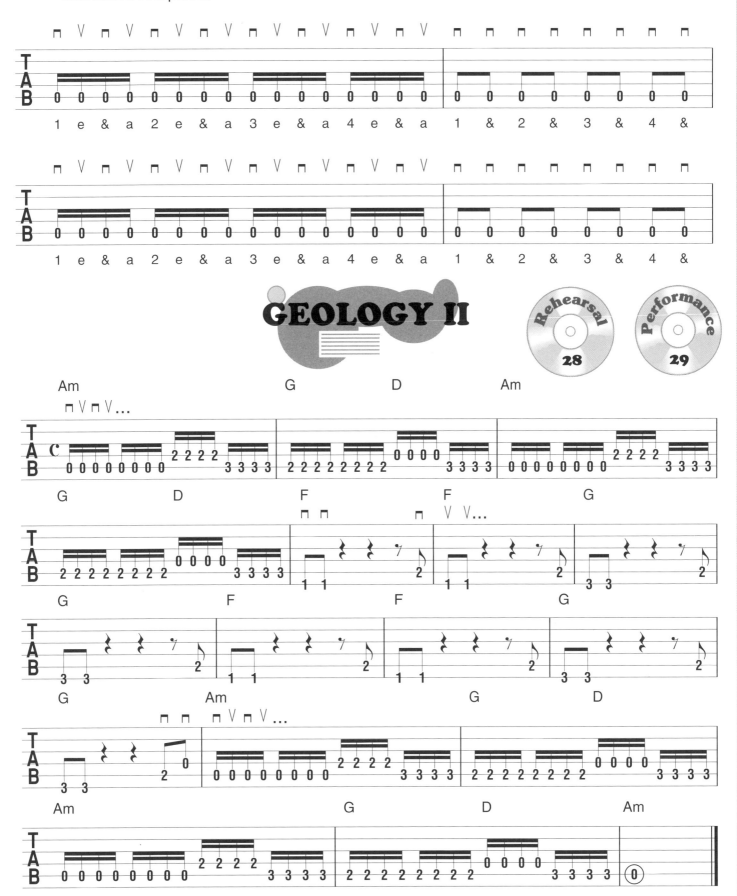

GEOLOGY II

Same But Different Rhythms

1 (e &) **a** 2 **&** (3   4)
With rests - choppy

1 e & **a**   2   **&** 3   4
With ties - smooth

PENTATONIC 2

Rehearsal 30   Performance 31

1 (e &) **a** 2 **&** (3)   **4** e & **a**...

1 e & **a** 2 **&** 3   4

OUT ON A LEDGER 2

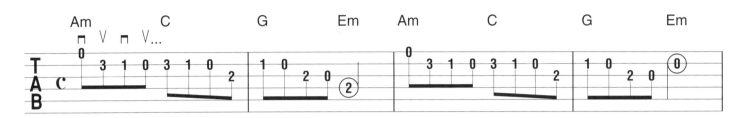

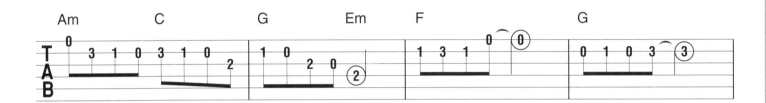

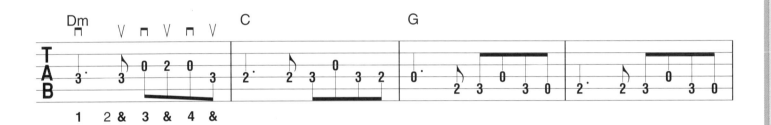

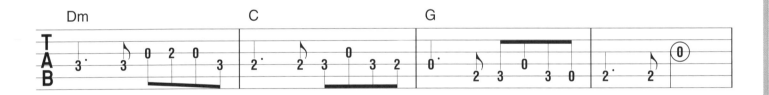

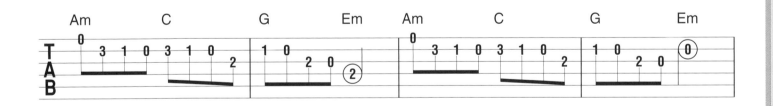

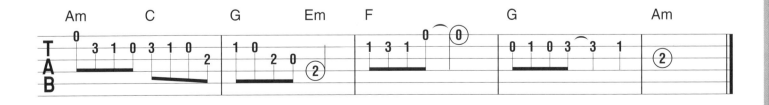

Major and Minor Scales

Try these scales with different rhythms (quarter notes, 8th notes, 16th notes and mixed.

Roots notes in black, example: ❸

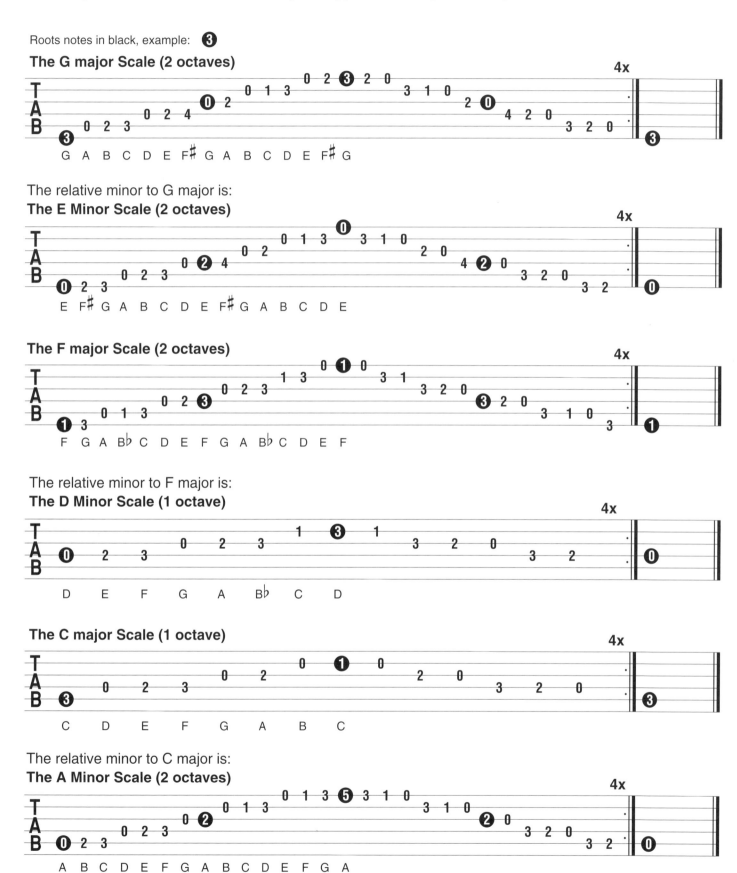

Major and Minor Pentatonic Scale Patterns

For better soloing we'll start on the low root note and play all the notes in each pattern above, below and back to the low root. Try with different rhythms (quarter notes, 8th notes, 16th notes and mixed).

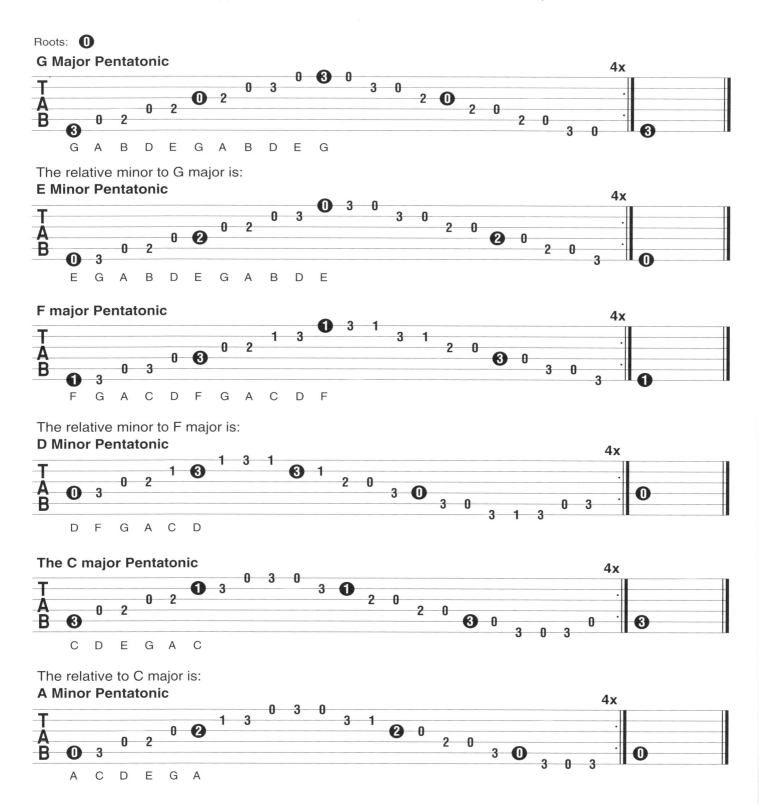

Guitar Solos

Here are some important ideas to keep in mind while improvising a guitar solo.

1. Which scale(s) to use – we will tell you for now.

2. Use parts of the melody in your solo.

3. Mix up the rhythms. Use whole, half, quarter, eighth, and 16th notes.
   It is also important to use rests.

4. Listen for good times to land on one of the root notes.

Scale to use - Em Pentatonic

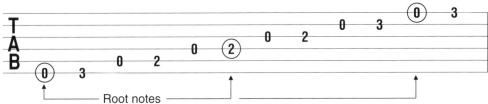

Root notes

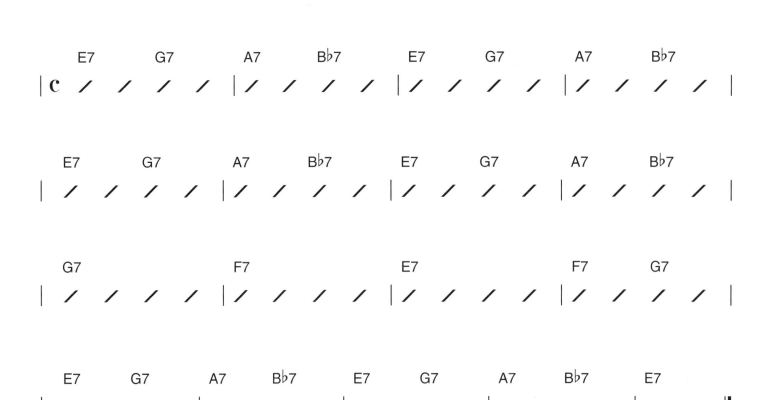

TWO DOWN SOLO

Scales to use:

Em Pentatonic

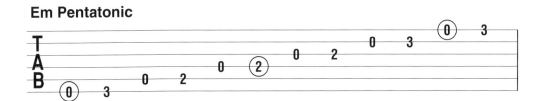

Em Scale

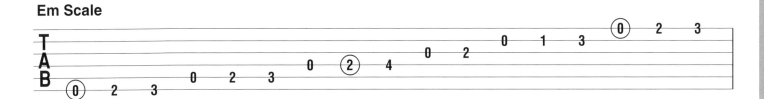

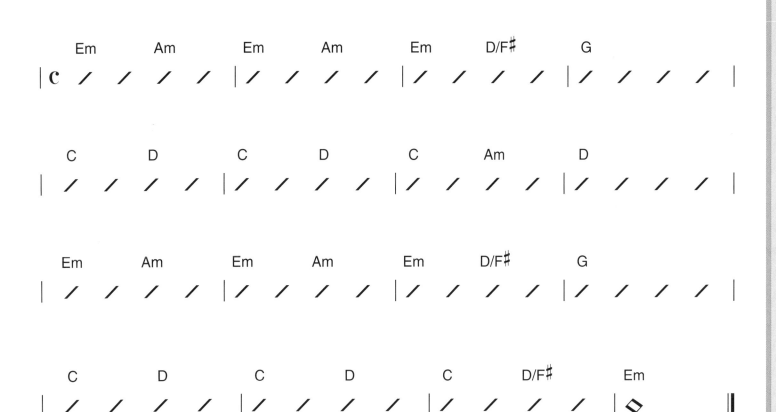

PHRYGIAN SEA (Solo)

Scales to use:

B Phrygian has the same notes as G Major except that the root note is considered "B" instead of "G."

G Major

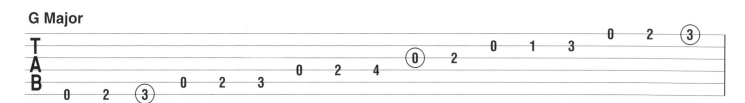

B Phrygian

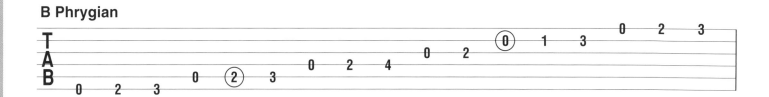

Use B Phrygian for this song.

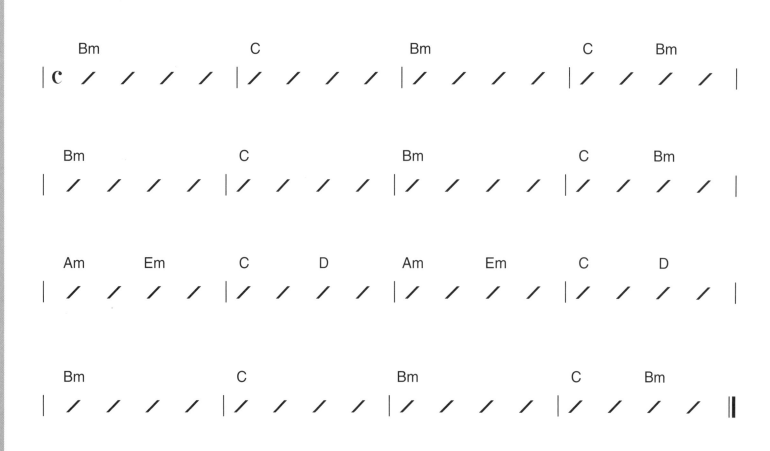

Scales to use:

G Major Pentatonic

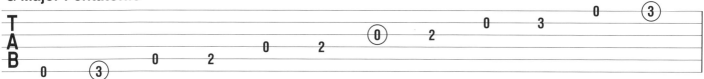

G Major Scale

FORTHRIGHT (Solo)

This song is in the key of D major but it also has chords in it from D minor. When this happens, the easiest scale to use is D minor pentatonic. There may be some notes that don't sound great with certain chords. So move away to different notes a quickly as possible.

Scale to use - Dm Pentatonic

OUT ON A LEDGER (Solo)

Scales to use:

A Minor Pentatonic

A Minor Scale

	Am	C	G	Em	Am	C	G	Em
C / / / /	/ / / /	/ / / /	/ / / /

	Am	C	G	Em	F		G	
	/ / / /	/ / / /	/ / / /	/ / / /

	Dm		C		G		
	/ / / /	/ / / /	/ / / /	/ / / /

	Dm		C		G		
	/ / / /	/ / / /	/ / / /	/ / / /

	Am	C	G	Em	Am	C	G	Em
	/ / / /	/ / / /	/ / / /	/ / / /

	Am	C	G	Em	F		G		Am
	/ / / /	/ / / /	/ / / /	/ / / /	◇

SURF STRING (Solo)

Scales to use:

E Minor Pentatonic

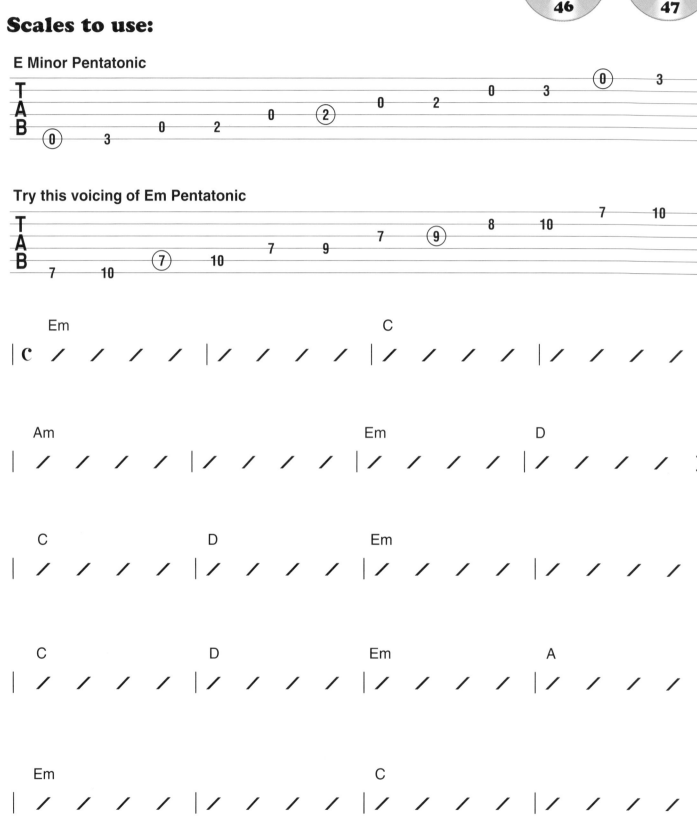

Try this voicing of Em Pentatonic

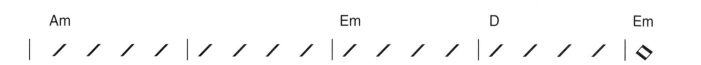

GEOLOGY II (Solo)

Scales to use:

A Minor Pentatonic

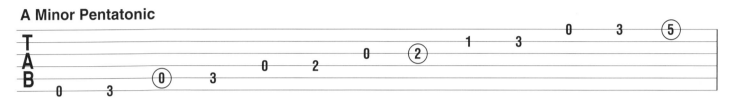

Try this voicing of A Minor Pentatonic

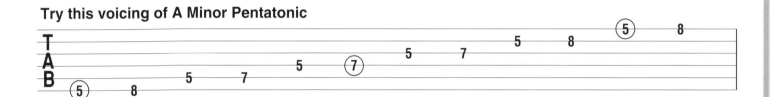

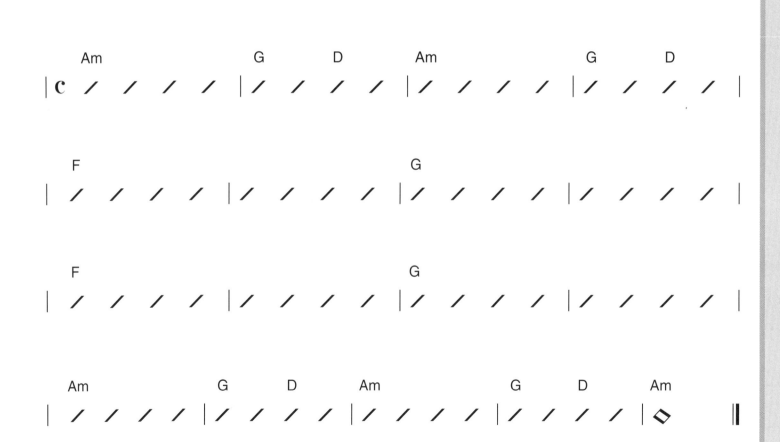

Congratulations! You are a lead guitarist!

Notes

```
T
A
B

T
A
B

T
A
B

T
A
B

T
A
B

T
A
B

T
A
B

T
A
B

T
A
B
```